Equal Opportunity
or More Opportunity?

Equal Opportunity
or More Opportunity?

The Good Thing About Discrimination

Richard A. Epstein

Commentary by

Simon Deakin

Civitas: Institute for the Study of Civil Society
London

First published March 2002

© The Institute for the Study of Civil Society 2002
The Mezzanine, Elizabeth House
39 York Road, London SE1 7NQ
email: books@civitas.org.uk

ISBN 1-903 386-18-7

Typeset by Civitas
in New Century Schoolbook

Printed in Great Britain by
The Cromwell Press
Trowbridge, Wiltshire

Contents

Authors

Richard A. Epstein is the James Parker Hall Distinguished Service Professor of Law at the University of Chicago, where he has taught since 1972, and since 2000, the Peter and Kirsten Bedford Senior Fellow at the Hoover Institution. He has been a member of the American Academy of Arts and Sciences since 1985 and a Senior Fellow of the Center for Clinical Medical Ethics at the University of Chicago Medical School since 1983. He served as editor of the *Journal of Legal Studies* from 1981 to 1991, and from 1991 to 2000 as an editor of the *Journal of Law and Economics*. He has been a Member of the California Bar from 1969 to the present. His books include *Torts* (Aspen Law & Business 1999); *Principles for a Free Society: Reconciling Individual Liberty with the Common Good* (Perseus Books, 1998); *Simple Rules for a Complex World* (Harvard, 1995); *Bargaining With the State* (Princeton, 1993); *Forbidden Grounds: The Case Against Employment Discrimination Laws* (Harvard, 1992); *Takings: Private Property and the Power of Eminent Domain* (Harvard, 1985); and *Modern Products Liability Law* (Greenwood Press, 1980).

Simon Deakin is Robert Monks Professor of Corporate Governance in the Judge Institute of Management and Yorke Professorial Research Fellow in the Faculty of Law at the University of Cambridge. After studying law at Cambridge he was a Bigelow Fellow at the University of Chicago Law School and subsequently a lecturer in London and Cambridge. He took up his present post in the autumn of 2001. His interests lie in the economics of law, and in particular employment, competition and company law. His books include *Contracts, Cooperation and Competition* (with Jonathan Michie), *Enterprise and Community* (with Alan Hughes) and *Labour Law* (with Gill Morris).

Foreword

Professor Richard Epstein argues that human rights laws, especially those designed to eliminate discrimination, do more harm than good. Many people who support laws against discrimination—whether on grounds of race, sex, disability or age—do so out of the best of intentions but Epstein believes they have over-estimated the ability of ⌐ laws to alter human conduct without producing unexpected results.

The classical liberal case against discrimination is that people should be judged by what they say and do, not their ascribed characteristics such as gender or the colour of their skin. If an employer is looking for someone to do a particular job, the sole concern should be the ability of candidates to carry out the expected tasks. With the exception of partisans of reverse discrimination, few would disagree. But, Epstein makes a further point that some will initially find shocking, namely that employers should be free to discriminate when racial or other distinctions are relevant to job performance. In truth, the claim that some discrimination is legitimate is not as shocking as it may seem, indeed it is acknowledged in British law that ethnic businesses, such as Chinese restaurants, can employ only Chinese waiters because to do otherwise would cast doubt on the authenticity of the restaurant.

Epstein believes that there are many complex situations in workplaces where it may simply be best for everyone if employers are allowed to pick new workers who will fit in with everyone else. This inevitably means that some employers will favour people from ethnic minorities and some will not. We spend a lot of our time at work and many of us naturally tend to mix with people we find congenial. Sometimes such preferences will be based on little more than sheer prejudice; and often idiosyncratic likes and dislikes will play their part. A wise employer who wants his staff to co-operate fully will take such factors into account. Personal animosity within a team can often impair the effectiveness of the organisation. For Epstein, the best way of handling these infinitely variable complexities is to allow employers and employees to enter into whatever contractual arrangements they wish.

To impose a legal requirement that treats any disproportionate representation of politically designated groups as evidence of discrimination leads to the making of false accusations against people who have done nothing more than to try to provide friendly working conditions for their staff in order to make it more likely they will do a good job and serve their customers well. The absurdities that can occur are already evident from American experience.

For example, a firm of cleaners in Chicago run by a Korean man largely recruited other Koreans, based on clan loyalty, just as many immigrants to America have relied on mutual aid among their own ethnic or national group. The owner was prosecuted by the Equal Employment Opportunity Commission (EEOC) because of the disproportionate representation of one ethnic group. He was pursued through the courts for over eight years at a cost of $200,000. In the end the owner won, but the cost forced the business to close. As a government agency, the EEOC had virtually unlimited resources and often pursued cases for which there was no legal precedent, calculating that it could coerce employers into making out-of-court settlements because they would think it a cheaper option. An innocent bystander could be excused for wondering whose interests were served by this policy.

Laws against racial discrimination are currently the most controversial. No reasonable person would be racist and, in a tolerant country like Britain, no reasonable person would want anyone else even to think they *might* be racist. For this reason we have bent over backwards to accommodate demands for anti-discrimination laws. But these laws have the opposite effect from the one claimed for them. They lead to race-conscious employment practices instead of the treatment of people according to their individual merits as fellow workers. Professor Epstein's remedy is to scrap current anti-discrimination law and replace it with a new form of words which recognises the value of legitimate differentiation. He suggests the following:

> Every individual and group may refuse to contract or associate with, or to otherwise discriminate for or against any other group or individual for whatever reasons they see fit, including without limitation, race, creed, sex, religion, age, disability, marital status, or sexual orientation. (p. 11)

The end result of such a reform would be an open society in which the common culture emerged from the free play of opinion. Some rules of life should be enforced by law, but in a free society many should be unenforceable, upheld only by social pressure following public discussion and experimentation.

Professor Epstein's study forms part of a wider Civitas project to encourage discussion of liberal anti-racism and to increase awareness of the dangers inherent in the authoritarian anti-racism that currently dominates public policy. Good intentions are rarely enough and Professor Epstein's study makes a compelling case for taking stock of prevailing attitudes.

Finally our thanks are due to three people who worked on this project as interns during 2001: Janet Ng, Laura Myers and Josie Cluer.

David G. Green

1

Human Rights and Anti-Discrimination Legislation

Human Rights Without Human Duties

It is easy to find strong similarities between British anti-discrimination laws and those in the United States. Indeed, laws of this type are increasingly popular elsewhere in Western democracies, and perhaps throughout the world, so that a comparison of these two systems carries with it wider implications. If I were to summarise my attitude to such laws in a single phrase, I would borrow the words originally used by Thomas Macaulay, perhaps inaccurately, in speaking about the US constitution—'all sail and no keel'. Macaulay meant that the constitution pulled people powerfully along, but lacked any countervailing forces to provide it with stability. If we run a boat on all sail and no keel, we put ourselves in peril. Anti-discrimination laws of the type now in force in Britain expose us dangerously to this problem—so much so that, in my view, the entire statutory apparatus should be scrapped.

Each of us is an individual. The rights we are trying to protect are only those belonging to ourselves. And rights matter. Three difficulties in particular are implicit in the general organisation and operation of anti-discrimination law.

It is salutary to compare current law with a famous civil rights statute in the United States—not the 1964 Civil

---

The first two chapters of this book are based on a lecture
'Restoring Sanctity of Contract in Employment
Relationships' given by Professor Epstein in Wellington,
New Zealand on 24 March 1999, and later published by
the New Zealand Business Roundtable, 1999.

Rights Act, but the 1866 statute of the same name which came after the long Civil War over slavery. The 1866 statute gave to all individuals rights such as the right to contract, to hold property, to convey real estate, to testify in court, and to sue or be sued. It essentially guaranteed civil capacity—the right to participate in a social order organised under the law of property, contract and tort. It was a civil rights act that primarily dealt with economic rights and liberties. Yet even here one must be careful to recognise and use 'economic' in the broadest sense, so that it covers all productive forms of human activities; the same principle that protected the ability to buy and sell wheat also protected the ability of people to marry whom they chose.

My second point follows on closely from the first. The 1866 statute, for example, is universal with respect to the rights that it affirms in all individuals. It says that every person shall have the right to contract, to dispose of property, and so forth. There is nothing in the statute that limits its benefits to some classes of individuals. Nor does it favour any side of a relationship by giving protection to one party and not to the other. It does not favour landlord over tenant, or employer over employee, or vice versa.

In this sense, the US Civil Rights Act 1964 is anything but a human rights statute, despite being labelled as such. In this Act, only certain individuals, occupying certain roles, can claim the protection of the statute, while other individuals, occupying other roles, are unambiguously subjected by law to certain correlative duties. The 1964 Civil Rights Act starts out by declaring it to be unlawful for an employer to engage in certain forms of discrimination. This places a limitation on an employer. There is no correlative duty or limitation placed on an employee: he or she can still discriminate in the choice of employer on the basis of any of the characteristics that are ruled out of bounds when it comes to an employer choosing an employee. This strongly suggests that the appropriate level of generality is found not in the modern statutes but in the 1866 statute. A meaningful human rights statute will surely protect all individuals equally, and equal protection of the laws (to refer to one clause of the Fourteenth Amendment adopted in 1868 in large part to give constitutional grounding to the 1866 Act) can be afforded only through some system of formal equality such as the 1866 Act provides.

There is a third, equally troublesome, feature of the modern statutes. Classical jurisprudence always insisted that human rights in some people came attached to human duties imposed on others. Rights were never free goods, but were paired with correlative duties; we always held a right against somebody else. To the extent that one person's liberty of action is expanded, the liberty of action of other individuals is necessarily limited. In designing a system of rights, the advantages that we conceive of and create for certain individuals should more than offset the disadvantages thereby imposed upon others. Any comprehensive system of rights should thus be couched within a framework that makes explicit the nature and extent of these correlative duties. A neutral presentation of a modern human rights law might entitle it the 'Human Rights and Duties Act', the consequences of which suddenly sound much less unambiguously positive. Opponents of the Act might even prefer to call it the 'Human Duties Act'—a title which does not draw our attention to the benefits associated with the statute, while wrongly suggesting that the Act merely sets out the duties of various individuals.

Once one recognises these three difficulties, certain other conclusions quickly follow. In particular, if we do not recognise—explicitly and publicly—the duties associated with rights, there will be an inherent tendency to ignore the associated costs. We will have the happy illusion that the constraints of scarcity do not really matter—that we will be able to magnify those rights without limitation while nobody need pay the cost either directly or indirectly. That is, of course, a fantasy.

How can such a fantasy take hold? Partly, I believe, through employing the following technique. Instead of talking in terms of human beings on both sides of the rights/duties divide, we depersonalise the nature of the entities on whom the duties are imposed. Individual people receive the benefits created by the statute, but its burdens are imposed on abstract entities such as corporations, unions, universities and other organisations. This mental conjuring trick cannot, of course, be justified. The collectives on which we impose duties are comprised of individuals. Organisations do not act themselves; they act through individuals and for individuals, be they shareholders, union members or faculty and students. Consequently, in analysing the impact of the statute we must always follow a postulate of methodological individualism. We cannot simply pair human rights to a set of correlative duties on abstract bodies, hoping thereby to externalise their costs on no one in particular. We must trace the implications of the statute through the entity to the particular individuals on whom those duties will be imposed. In politics the same principle applies. It is meaningless to say that the government has a 'duty' to supply benefits to its citizens. Any benefits created by the government must necessarily be backed by regulation, taxation or the imposition of liability on other individuals. Those burdens must be recognised and weighed against the benefits, if an appropriate balance is to be obtained. And we can be sure that this balance will not be obtained if public rhetoric suppresses information on the incidence and expense from the relevant trade-offs.

Moreover, when the cost elements of a modern human rights statute are allowed to enter into any equation, they are never placed on the same footing as the rights side. It is characteristic of these statutes that the rights are put, so to speak, in bold 16-point type at the top of the page while underneath and on one side in barely legible 8-point type are the costs. If the costs turn out to be too great, they may not even feature at all. The almost universal tendency is thus to underestimate the costs, because they do not enter simultaneously into the calculations as an inescapable correlative duty. Instead, they are superimposed upon the general system only as an afterthought. We can have 'rights' that are extraordinarily costly for other individuals, and instead of treating them as infringements of ordinary liberties we treat them as the price that must be paid to enforce some outcome which is seen as self-evidently desirable.

There is a further paradox associated with modern human rights legislation. If the specified rights are those most fundamental to human liberties, why have they taken so long in historical terms to come on to the forefront of the legislative agenda? Their introduction dates only from the 1960s. They are not the issues over which wars were fought back in the thirteenth century. Nor are they the factors most people would regard as truly fundamental for their own well-being and security. If I were asked to choose, for example, between the various modern prohibitions of discrimination, and the common law prohibition against the use of force against other individuals, I have no doubts whatsoever as to which set of rights I would discard. I would allow people to refuse to deal with me in situations such as employment, so long as I believed that the state was around to protect my bodily integrity. I doubt that in any real-world setting one could find even a single person who would choose differently. Nobody would prefer the risk of being killed—no matter how 'non-discriminatory' the slaughter—to a general rule prohibiting the use of force. Such a rule promotes the security of us all, even at the expense of some liberty which we would all willingly sacrifice for the gains we obtain by demanding like sacrifices of others.

Yet what about a closer comparison? The modern statutory rights that guarantee freedom from discrimination with those which allow persons to make contracts to dispose of their labour or property? Here a moment's reflection should indicate that the basic right to trade occupies the more fundamental position. That right is critical to survival no matter what the structure of the marketplace. To deny people the right to trade is to force them to rely exclusively on their own resources and to negate the enormous benefits of the division of labour. Seen in this light, the anti-discrimination norm is heavily parasitic on the basic right to trade. An anti-discrimination norm may be of some assistance in a world of strict monopolies, but it makes far less sense in competitive labour markets, where individuals have a multiplicity of options from which to choose. So here again the basic economic right has, and should enjoy, a priority over the anti-discrimination rules embodied in the modern laws.

Aspiration and Performance

The preceding argument put matters as an 'either/or' proposition. But what about the possibility of recognising *both* the traditional economic rights and the newer anti-discrimination law? Part of the difficulty with that position is that the two systems are inconsistent with each other, as the former gives persons the absolute right of choice of their trading partners that the latter denies. We can find places where the duty not to discriminate makes sense, mainly in connection with a monopoly provider of standardised services, such as electricity and gas. Here the utter lack of consumer choice requires the holder of that franchise to take all comers. But most labour markets, for example, bear no resemblance to this situation, yet it is precisely in this context that they hope to use law to eradicate all vestiges of discrimination.

What the advocates of human rights often overlook, however, is the important distinction between the morality of obligation and the morality of aspiration. Of course, we want individuals to treat all other persons fairly and with dignity and respect.

But it hardly follows that legal tools should be used to enforce these higher duties. We should be cautious about imbuing the morality of aspiration with near-religious overtones. We have to worry about the dangers of implementation as well. I do not wish to be vicious, mean or nasty to other people. That is not the object of any of us. But the legal system should have certain spheres of influence and social systems should have others. Typically we start off with some coercive programme that looks noble and lofty, but by the time we appreciate all of its implications we run the risk of descending into some form of Orwellian madness.

The unanticipated friction and dislocation that takes place as a result of the statute means that the aspirations are never realised, but rather the opposite occurs.

Let us talk about disability. No one wants disabled people to rot at home. But it is implementation that matters. There are two ways to handle the disability issue. First, in any job market some employers will be niche firms which will specialise in hiring people with disabilities. Before the United States adopted its anti-discrimination legislation, some employers acquired certain types of facilities such as ramps or reading machines (depending on the disability they were dealing with), amortised them across large numbers of employees with disabilities and traded profitably in specialised markets. To spur on that activity, the government could subsidise with block grants firms that hired workers with certain types of disabilities. There is no need to use command-and-control tactics when these approaches are available. *grants*

There is no panacea, for even block grants have coercive elements. These grants must be financed out of taxation. Yet it is possible to choose even among different types of coercive legal regimes. Taxation is an explicit, overt burden which can be quantified. Regulations are hidden and unquantifiable, but they often impose a larger tax. If we are forcing employers to hire workers with disabilities we are taxing right now. The question is whether taxation should be overt or concealed; whether public expenditures should be 'transparent' or 'off-budget'. The academic literature on taxation and regulation and their substitute relationship has been well established for the last 25 years. It is only in a political context that the two are treated as if they are in different moral domains. If we understand regulation as imposing a burden upon one group for the benefit of another, we can duplicate that by taxing the first group and transferring the wealth to the second. We can choose either to quantify the costs publicly and expose them for responsible political debate or to bury them in a form of regulation overblown by a rhetoric of rights. I opt for the first approach.

There is yet a second vice to the human rights approach. It makes it appear as though our sole concern with disabilities should be confined to helping people who already suffer from disability. That is too narrow a point of view, for it is also of evident importance to prevent as many people as possible from becoming handicapped. One effective way to do that is to raise the general standard of living so people will have more resources to keep out of harm's way. But we cannot raise standards of living with an economically crippling human rights statute: by raising production costs and distorting business decisions, it lowers per capita incomes. An explicit tax surely has costs in this regard, but precisely because it is explicit it is less likely to be disruptive. And it is less likely to be commandeered by administrative agencies who attach pride of place to their own mission, disregarding everything else. We should not be fooled by an abstract argument that we need such a statute for a just, kind, and compassionate society. All of us can be just, kind and compassionate without governmental instruction.

An Alternative Approach to Civil Rights

The dangers of the common form of human rights legislation should encourage us to develop some alternative conception of human rights. Here I reveal myself as an unabashed and unashamed classical liberal who believes the modern definition of human rights is a rhetorical ploy and a mistake. Any soundly based system of rights must have the appropriate level of universality and must recognise the dual and correlative nature of rights and obligations. I am confident that we can find a better legal framework.

In my own formulation, all individuals are owners of themselves, and of those resources they can acquire either through original possession or through contract and exchange with other individuals. There is nothing people care about which cannot fall under the class of either labour or property, including the crucial right to associate with other individuals, be it for commercial, social or religious reasons. This gives us a broad definition untroubled by the ambiguity of modern statutes.

Such a system meets our first concern, because it is general and comprehensive. Nor is this system merely a form of class legislation disguised under the veneer of human rights. This is not a statute that guarantees rights to employees against employers, tenants against landlords, buyers against sellers, or customers against their banks and insurance companies. It merely gives all individuals the right to dispose of and control their own labour—which is their personal liberty—and their own property in any way, and under any circumstances, that they see fit, subject to the exception for monopoly providers noted above. Since it extends to other forms of association and expression, it covers a broader domain of behaviour than does a human rights statute geared only to the employment arrangement. Even with its greater scope of influence, it still guarantees a degree of formal equality that contemporary human rights statutes lack. To be sure, formal equality will never guarantee perfect social equality. But it is a dangerous illusion to think we guarantee social equality by a statute which systematically violates the requirements of formal equality. We are better advised to promote liberty, without attempting to introduce class legislation. It gives us a system that is self-contained and universal in the safeguards it provides to all individuals.

When we come to the question of how correlative duties are to be incorporated, my classical liberal system also compares well with its modern competitor. For any given right, the obligations on the other side are clearly defined. To the extent that individuals exercise their personal liberties, they must refrain from taking actions that interfere with other individuals. This applies to the way in which they run their own lives, enter into voluntary exchanges, and utilise or dispose of their property. And it carries over to religious and social organisations as well. My system must pass the test as to whether, under these circumstances, the security we each gain from the protection of our rights over our own person and property is worth more to us than the ability to restrict those liberties when they are vested in other people.

The answer under these circumstances is unambiguous. To the extent that we create individual rights over persons and property, we have given an initial set of endowments to the people who most value and know how to use them, be it for production, consumption or spiritual reflection. No human rights commission can dictate what is relevant to my own preferences, or to the way in which I think and act in the world. It is a vast mistake to assume that I—or anybody else—have a cache of legitimate information that allows me, or you, to set the preferences and control the choices of other individuals. Something is of value to an individual if it enhances his or her utility, which is subjectively determined. In my system, the protection given to other individuals is a powerful one: if they do not agree with my conceptions of value they can choose to associate or trade only with other individuals. They can leave me alone, just as I can leave them alone. Under this model there is a series of initial entitlements which, in a series of voluntary exchanges, people can use and combine in any number of mutually advantageous ways: they can deal with one or with many, and they can engage in short-term exchanges or long-term exchanges as they see fit. We can then have an indefinite number of such arrangements, relationships and exchanges. Under this system of free contracting and free association we get the best division of labour, and the best redeployment of human and natural resources for the full range of individual and social ends. The system that starts in commerce can easily go beyond it to all forms of personal associations. In the long run this comprehensive system will greatly outperform any system of command and control in which people are told what they can do and how they can do it. The rejection of the modern approach to human rights quickly has broader implications.

A Short, Sensible Civil Rights Statute

It is perfectly possible to draft on a single page a statute giving a comprehensive definition of all rights and duties for all individuals. The statute is designed to cover all the employment issues of modern human rights legislation, but to go beyond them to cover questions of freedom of association more generally. With a little more ingenuity it could deal with such matters as monopoly and freedom of expression more generally. And this enactment is not directed towards the criminal law, including the requirements of a hearing with notice of charges before an impartial tribunal. But over its chosen contractual and associational domain, this statute can be understood by anyone of ordinary intelligence in a relatively short time. It requires no special administrative agencies or elaborate tribunals to enforce its rules, nor do those rules have an *ad hoc* quality. Here is the complete statute.

Human Rights Act, Revised

S1. Every individual and group shall, in the use and disposition of property or labour, have the right to contract, associate or otherwise transact or do business with any other individual or group whom they choose on whatever terms and conditions they see fit, and for whatever purposes they see fit, be they commercial, social or religious.

S2. Every individual and group may refuse to contract or associate with, or to otherwise discriminate for or against any other group or individual for whatever reasons they see fit, including without limitation, race, creed, sex, religion, age, disability, marital status, or sexual orientation.

S3. (a) Every individual or group may ask of any other individual or group any question they see fit, no matter how offensive, impertinent, illegitimate, superficial or irrelevant.
(b) Every individual or group may refuse to answer any question, however tactful, pertinent, legitimate, insightful, or relevant.

S4. (a) Every agreement, contract, or association shall be construed in accordance with the ordinary meanings of its terms, as informed by custom and common usage within the relevant trade, industry, or social or religious grouping.

(b) No construction or interpretation of any agreement, contract, or articles of association shall be made or influenced by principles of unconscionability, adhesion, inequality of bargaining power, *contra proferentem,* or any other rule that presumes one party to the agreement or contract enjoys a protected or preferred social status relative to the other.

S5. Every individual or group shall have the right to offer transportation or other services for hire on the public highways, waterways or in the public airspace, subject only to reasonable and nondiscriminatory regulations imposed in the interest of public safety.

S6. All actions brought to enforce rights under any contract, agreement or association shall be commenced in the County Court. The Commission for Racial Equality, the Equal Opportunities Commission, the Disability Rights Commission, Employment Tribunals, the ..., the ..., and the ... are hereby abolished.

The Two Approaches Compared

United States anti-discrimination laws give rise to problems at least as grave as those found in Britain. The American laws have been in place for longer, and our administrative apparatus has grown in power and influence at every level and layer of government.

To facilitate our comparison, consider first how information will be generated and transmitted in any market. In my own proposed model the process is quite simple. One person can ask another person any question at all. That party can decline to answer, and thus refuse to give the information that the questioner seeks and believes is relevant. If the questioner receives no reply, she is faced with a choice: she can simply accept that she does not have that information, or she can put the same question to somebody else who may be willing to answer it. By these simple interplays between individuals, the right amount of information will tend to be generated about factors that are relevant to certain long-term contracts, whether they be for employment or for the sale of property. In this system there is no external measure of relevance: there is simply an interchange between two parties to decide what they care about and how it will be provided.

This system deals much more powerfully than alternative systems with one of the major criticisms of markets which are used to justify state action. It is often said that people cannot make rational choices where there is incomplete information. But anti-discrimination law has the state taking exactly the wrong approach by forcing people to be 'blind' about issues that matter to their own welfare. Anti-discrimination law is the complete opposite to a full disclosure statute such as we have in securities law (which I also believe to be a mistake because of its mandatory nature). The 'informed choices' that we prefer people to make become 'uninformed choices', because the legislation deprives people of information they would regard as relevant, even if the state does not. The conclusion from standard theory on markets and information is that the factors regarded by anti-discrimination as irrelevant for decision making are in fact highly relevant, indeed critical. British law is heading full bore in the wrong direction.

Age is a good example. Nobody can doubt that age is relevant to certain decisions as to whether or not to hire a person for a certain job. We think about age when we contemplate marriage, for all the obvious reasons. Similar obvious reasons apply with respect to jobs. An organisation hiring individuals is not just hiring them for the immediate period to which the initial contract of employment applies. It is attempting to hire people who will also be with the organisation years—or even decades—down the track. In so doing, it will be attempting to amortise the costs of hiring and training a person over the expected period of the employment relationship. If we are hiring somebody in the context of a 20-year time frame, a 58-year-old person (like me) will clearly expose us to much greater retirement risk and mortality risk than a much younger person. We will be less likely to recover our investment over the life of the contract. We act rationally when we decide that this particular position should be awarded to someone else.

In many circumstances, then, rational decisions about the use of human capital and long-term employment contracts necessarily require information about age. When statutes here and in the United States lay down that age is irrelevant and prevent mandatory retirement, they are effectively saying that somebody in the government knows so much about the workings of business that they can tell every firm adopting a contrary practice that they are wrong-headed. The implicit proposition is that all of these firms have failed to understand some hidden moral imperative or practical economic argument in structuring their employment arrangements. It is one thing merely to be wrong in particular cases. No system, no management team functions perfectly, no matter what the incentive structure. But it is quite another thing to be wrong system-wide, without possibility of correction, which is what happens when the statute asserts a monopoly over wisdom, and forces everybody else to follow its dictates against their own better judgment.

It would be a mistake to assume that older workers are always harmed by discriminatory policies. It is easy to identify other reasons why firms may want to discriminate by age—reasons that run in the opposite direction. A firm may wish to hire people with experience, or people of a certain age, because they will be more compatible with the firm's customer base. Under some circumstances, the person aged 35 may be unsuitable to the job and the person aged 58 highly desirable. It is mistaken for the law to assume that, if people acquire information on age, they will always use it toward the end of excluding older people. The reality is entirely more nuanced and complex. What people are looking for has nothing to do with discrimination in the invidious sense, but with fit. If individuals are allowed to pair up on that basis we will see higher employment and output, because the matching of people to jobs will be more appropriate to the tastes and temperaments of individuals. The more one understands about human resource economics, the more apparent it becomes that every single characteristic regarded as irrelevant under anti-discrimination law may in some settings be absolutely critical for the intelligent deployment of resources. One cannot have a 100 per cent error rate by chance. Results that are bad come only when the initial premise is itself faulty.

I have thus far argued that anti-discrimination law is so misconceived that it is pointing in precisely the wrong direction. Relaxing the prohibition on age would not be an attempt to switch the advantage from old to young, or from young to old. It would be a move designed to achieve a better fit between jobs and the people who fill them. Anyone who works in management will tell you that fit, morale and cohesiveness are critical to the culture of an organisation. Yet these 'soft' features—so important to the operation of markets—are ignored by a blunderbuss statute that paradoxically takes a highly atomistic view of an employee's 'merit' that is routinely rejected in market settings. That truncated view of fit survives only on the false premise that some omniscient being knows how every institution should run, from a small shop to a large manufacturing corporation. The statute is an example of the one-suit-fits-all mentality that is so destructive of productive human relationships.

The discordant element in the British anti-discrimination law relates to the tendency of enforcement agencies to worry so little about costs relative to benefits. It is simply not plausible to assume that a person who is involved full-time in a business, with incentives to examine every conceivable option to make the business run better, can overlook measures which would be to the advantage of his own company, while somebody who looks at it from the outside, without any financial responsibility whatsoever, and with all sorts of implicit biases based upon a different institutional agenda, will get it right. I am not arguing that firms are always right and regulators always wrong. I am arguing that it is absurd to suggest that a regulator second-guessing the commercial decisions of a company will do that task as well, over the long run, as the company itself. We should play the sensible odds.

I believe that my own one-page statute meets, at least as a first approximation, the requirements of a human rights law in a much simpler and cheaper fashion than the current system. If somebody does not like this statute, can they improve upon it? Can they justify the hundreds of millions of pounds in foregone economic efficiency that will be required to run an alternative system? I think not. It is important, too, to understand what my alternative statute really means. It does not say that we like, invite, encourage or celebrate stupid, ignorant, foolish, invasive and impertinent questions. Rather, it effectively says that if we allow individuals to choose the questions they are legally entitled to ask, the incentives they face will lead them to ask what in practice turn out to be the most relevant types of questions. They will tend to discriminate in ways that are productive rather than invidious. In fact one advantage of the statute is that it makes it far easier for people to adopt voluntary affirmative action programmes if they so choose, without having to explain to others why they choose to do so. In light of this option, we cannot conclude that this is a statute that announces we have no moral sense and no social conscience. It merely says that our legal rules should be those that are relatively lean with respect to what we require of other individuals, and that the set of social sanctions which are informally developed and articulated can, at far lower cost, deal with repugnant forms of conduct. Any contest between the alternative package and my single page is like a battle between a 1942 vacuum tube special and today's integrated circuits on a chip, in terms of their capacity to deliver services relative to the cost of the product.

I am of course aware that certain recurrent objections will be raised against this position. For example, it will be said that this simple statute presupposes that markets are perfect when of course we know that they are not. No one should believe that markets, even competitive markets, are perfect instruments of social policy. But the question of imperfection cuts both ways. If markets are imperfect institutions, then legislation is also imperfect. We must make an assessment of the relative size of the imperfections, given the incentives under which people operate in both settings. To the extent that individuals have both self-interest and information about themselves, they are correspondingly better judges of their desires, and better judges of what they are willing to sacrifice in order to obtain those desires. Any system of regulation with compassion must be able to provide people with what they want. How can regulators know what people want? Legislation ostensibly designed to benefit one group can end up harming another. For example, curb cuts will help people in wheelchairs, but make it harder for people who are blind. We need to be very aware of the situation on both sides before we can be sure whether we are helping individuals.

Similarly, self-interest is a force to be reckoned with in all legal orders from the nightwatchman state to the planned economy. Viewed abstractedly, self-interest may become a destructive force or it may be immensely creative. Which outcome dominates generally depends on the incentive structure that surrounds the self-interest. It is very easy to talk about such things as market failures, monopoly and information problems, but it is equally critical to recognise and discuss candidly the failures of democratic systems: capture, faction, intrigue and special interest. Never assume away public choice difficulties and the perverse outcomes that can flow from any ambitious legal programmes.

2

Age Discrimination
and Employment Law

The topic of discrimination in the law of employment is
one of the growth industries of our time. The issue
covers the gamut from race, to sex, disability and age. This
last category is perhaps the most important because the
dogged insistence that age be disregarded or de-emphasised
in employment decisions cuts against the grain of the
employment policy of virtually every well managed private
firm. As an outsider, I will try to place the overarching
issues in a wider international context. The problems
surrounding anti-discrimination laws are far from unique
to Britain and afflict many other countries, including the
United States.

Contrasting Philosophies in the Labour Market

What is the most appropriate form of regulation to govern
the employment relationship? It should be stressed that I
am not advocating some anarcho-capitalist system in which
the law takes absolutely no interest in employment contracts. The serious debate has always been between those
who believe that the primary function of employment law is
to respect the contractual terms emerging from a market
transaction and to enforce those terms with the aim of
providing contracts with greater stability, and those who
believe that some of the contractual terms emerging from
negotiations will be distorted or biased in ways that call for
legal redress.

While some anti-discrimination measures are clearly
misconceived, it does not follow that we should proceed
automatically to a system of completely free contracting in

the labour market. We might still wish to impose some specific limitations on contractual freedom. Indeed there are reasons rooted in the common law not to enforce certain contracts, although most are relatively unimportant in the context of labour law. For instance, we need not concern ourselves with contracts designed to kill or maim third persons. Nor are we troubled by violations of antitrust or competition policy, which almost by definition cannot arise in individual contracts between employers and employees. Thus we face no problems arising from the external effects of contracts that might lead a legal system to deny their enforcement.

We might also choose not to enforce a contract if there has been some defect in the bargaining process. But a striking feature of employment contracts is that they are typically not tainted by fraud or duress. There are rarely any hidden or surprising conditions associated with them, and certainly none that requires a system-wide public response. On the contrary, employment contracts are designed to facilitate long-term relationships. People undertake their jobs day in and day out. At least after a while, they have good knowledge of their working conditions. In these settings, with fairly full information, wages and other key terms of employment contracts are not likely to cause unfair surprise.

To the extent that sudden and unpleasant surprises do occur and alter the expectations on which a contract is based, the typical reaction is readily anticipated. Workers who find themselves short-changed in one job will simply leave for greener pastures elsewhere. It is this ability to quit—and the consequent cost to a firm of finding and training a replacement—which constrains employers in the labour market so efficiently. It is easy to overlook the advantages that a contract at will has for employees.

Open Markets Penalise Irrational Discrimination

Adherents to the interventionist philosophical tradition have attempted to counter the movement towards a more liberal labour market. One part of their tradition is the legislation known as anti-discrimination laws in the United States. These laws are based on the assumption that employers are so irrational, so prejudiced and so unwise that they will turn down well-qualified applicants simply because they are blinded by some antiquated prejudice. In considering applications, employers find there are a wide variety of grounds that they are simply forbidden to take into account. Criteria such as race or sex have long been favourites for legislators in this tradition, while more recently grounds such as sexual orientation, disability and age have been added to the list.

In reality, the basic argument for freedom of contract is so strong that it leaves no role for anti-discrimination laws. While such a view is easily defended, it is regarded as very radical in some quarters. On a recent visit to New Zealand, I defended the free contracting position in a debate with the chief human rights commissioner, Pamela Jefferies, in a way that she found rather shocking. But when analysing prejudice in employment markets, people such as Ms Jefferies make the mistake of assuming that markets are like politics. In politics there is one outcome that applies to everyone, and it tends to be determined by the attitudes and behaviour of the median voter. But the sentiments of a market are not uniformly determined by some 'average' or 'median' participant. There may be a market in which large numbers of people harbour all sorts of irrational and offensive prejudices. Yet as long as there is some segment of that market where people can be hired on the strength of their qualifications and ability to do a job, wages will not be lower in that sector. In economic terms, the important persons are those who operate at the margin, not those in the middle of the pack. Provided there is open entry, any good worker who is temporarily neglected in one section of the market will find alternative employment elsewhere.

Of course, it may take some time before individual firms respond to competitive pressures. But ultimately a firm's prejudices will rebound to harm the firm more than the people it refused to hire. After all, it is simply not good business to refrain from hiring women or blacks on the basis of some irrational dislike of these groups. Once firms appreciate that fact, prejudices do not last very long by cutting off access to a low-cost supply of high-quality labour. Thus, if we observe persistent discrimination in some form, we should not automatically assume it is bad. Rather than banning it, we should ask ourselves why such discrimination might make sense in terms of the specific employment relationship. And before considering the legislative alternative, we should recognise that the rigidities that banning discrimination will produce in the end will increase the employer's search costs and the switching time for workers and employers alike. The positive search costs that discrimination may create are not simply eliminated by an anti-discrimination law, even one that is responsibly administered. Any 'for cause' requirement for hiring and firing will necessarily slow the time for hiring and force qualified applicants to jump (if not trip) over another set of hurdles.

The Special Case of Age Discrimination

Given these general observations, I think it would be a mistake to assume all anti-discrimination laws have an equal impact on the day-to-day operation of the market. It is worth stressing that the most dangerous of all the human rights laws is potentially the prohibition on age discrimination. The reason hearkens back to my opening observations. In the absence of any human rights law, very few firms would have an explicit policy of saying 'no women welcome here', or 'no blacks welcome here', or 'no Jews welcome here'. That is not a clever way to attract business: in attracting a few people, the firm would guarantee that hundreds more would stay away. It would have worked a public relations wonder in reverse.

But the practice regarding age discrimination is very different. Before the introduction of the anti-discrimination statutes in the United States, chief executives in their mid-50s were putting in place mandatory retirement policies for themselves and everybody else on their staff, including the senior staff with the greatest economic influence and power. If this practice was widespread, why should we assume collective irrationality in this part of the market? The answer is not that these business people were stupid and failed to understand the consequences of their decisions. The only parties that failed to understand the consequences were the legislatures that passed these statutes. Ironically, it is the defenders of anti-discrimination laws who often accuse me of being out of touch. Time and again I am told: 'You cannot talk intelligently about labour relationships, Professor Epstein, because you have never been in business or managed a workforce. You are only a university professor, locked away in your ivory tower.' I fully accept the charge that I am ignorant about how many individual business people run their firms. But that is precisely the point. Suppose somebody in a legislature has actually worked in one job, at one place, at one time prior to taking public office. They now have (or, perhaps, had) an intimate knowledge of perhaps a handful of people in a particular business, whether in London or Chicago. What makes that person so confident about how to figure out the best employment policies for everybody else in Britain, the United States, or anywhere else?

The whole point about markets is that each of us has knowledge that only encompasses a very small part of the world around us. Whenever I hear politicians speak about universities, I take a deep breath. Indeed my knowledge of the University of Chicago does not translate easily into a working knowledge of its peer institutions. Similarly, if business people heard me pontificating about how they should organise their production lines or computer systems, they would breathe just as deeply. The point is that neither my views nor those of anyone else should rule absolutely in all factories and offices. If business people decide that a mandatory retirement age is not appropriate in their own business, they can eliminate it voluntarily. If they believe some extremely talented person should be exempt from a mandatory retirement rule, they can make that case to their chief executive. The fact that mandatory retirement rules have been in place over long periods of time suggests not that these policies are silly, but rather that they have a rationale sufficiently powerful to command broad support among businesses operating in a wide range of industries. Our job is to understand what that rationale is.

Naïve Assumptions By the Regulators

The proponent of an anti-discrimination statute typically comes forward with a smooth and reassuring speech. 'We are eliminating arbitrariness in business', it goes. 'Arbitrariness is of course bad, and we are replacing it with a principle with which everybody agrees. We are simply requiring all employers to assess individual workers solely on their ability to do their job at any given time. Outmoded employment policies are replaced with merit assessments. Who is against merit?' Strangely enough, at this point nobody raises a hand. It is like asking whether anyone is against motherhood. The proposal is made to sound so reasonable that anyone who has been doing something different is by implication too ignorant to understand the strength of this progressive new idea.

However, the argument can only take this form if we make a particularly naïve assumption about social behaviour: that one change in a legal rule leads to only one change in social consequences. Thus, if we eliminate the mandatory retirement policy by legislation, everything else in the firm is expected to continue exactly as before. There will simply be splendid new merit-based assessments in place of the old policies, which were arbitrary and worthless. Businesses will be better off (despite having opposed the statute) and nobody will be worse off. Who can resist such an alluring outcome?

Unfortunately, similar arguments have been made in other contexts and have always been proved wrong. For instance, the attention of legislators too often falls on the minimum wage law. For them, raising the minimum wage can only have one consequence: it will raise to a new minimum level the wages of workers who were below that level, and nothing else will change. In reality, we know there will be other consequences. If the price of labour (i.e. the wage rate) rises, the quantity of labour employed by firms will fall, leading to a rise in unemployment. While the empirical studies show that the employment losses from the minimum wage are not quite as high as simple theory would predict, this does not mean that the negative consequences are not as great as claimed. It merely shows that the simple theory failed to incorporate all the other ways for firms to adjust their behaviour at the margin.

For instance, a firm might continue to employ the same number of workers after a rise in the minimum wage, but no longer provide free training. Instead it might require workers to enrol in training classes at their own expense before being hired. Or a firm that had given its workers the convenience of single shifts might now demand split shifts. Or it might now require its workers to purchase their own uniforms or equipment, rather than pay for them itself. There are hundreds of different ways in which the employment relationship can change. The idea that altering a single variable like the minimum wage will leave all other variables unchanged simply defies the laws of economics. It is like a chemist saying that salt can be added to a solution without changing the concentration of sodium and chlorine ions. Everything is elaborately interconnected. Any important perturbation to the system will have powerful consequences in many directions over the long term.

Exactly the same logic operates in the case of age-discrimination laws. We must ask ourselves: 'If we push here, where will the bulge appear? What changes will take place, and why?' To answer those questions we need to consider why many firms had mandatory retirement rules in the first place. There are a variety of reasons. Some concern the relationship between the individual employee and the firm. Others concern the overall composition of a firm's workforce and its desire to keep its stock of human capital deployed over time in a reasonably coherent fashion.

Younger Workers Learn Faster

Let us consider first individual workers. An ongoing problem for any firm is how to train its workers for tasks they will be performing in the future. It is a great illusion, to which academics are not immune, to imagine that only schools and universities provide education. Firms in fact supply huge amounts of training to their workers in various ways. Sometimes they take their workers for a weekend retreat where they teach them new computer systems. Other times it can be on-the-job instruction. When a firm makes investments in education and training, two features associated with the return from those investments are of obvious concern.

One is how quickly the new knowledge is absorbed by the relevant employees. Compared with my sons in their teens, I am a person with ten thumbs when it comes to learning new computer skills. They are simply much more adept at picking up modern technology than I am. I am clearly not alone in this predicament: after all the common joke is, if you don't understand your new computer, have your ten-year-old explain it all to you. Thus, when it comes to assimilating new types of information, people should recognise that younger employees can have very powerful advantages.

These differential abilities do not pass unnoticed in business. When investing in its workers, a firm faces certain decisions. It wants its older workers to keep performing those tasks that they do well. But it will probably not select those workers for training and development when new ventures and promising lines of innovation are involved. It is one of those truths that everyone knows but few people are prepared to acknowledge: flexibility and plasticity diminish with age, not in all cases, but surely on average. A large percentage of older workers are set in ways that are not easily altered or undone. Employers know from practical experience that it is true, and the fact that some politician dares them to state the obvious should not justify their remaining silent. They should plainly point out that the ability to learn new tricks is different at different age levels. This means that, on average, the responses of older persons will at some stage, and for some roles, be inferior.

There is a line of cases in the United States involving airline pilots who had been forced to retire as pilots at age

60 by the Federal Aviation Authority. When the time for retirement arrived, the pilots insisted on their right to be trained as flight engineers. So these 60-year-olds, who had been pilots all their lives, were put on the same training courses as navigation engineers in their mid-20s. It was as though these 60-year-olds simply could not learn. They slowed up the classes, but they could not handle the procedures; they were absolutely hopeless students. Yet they had been fine pilots, which demonstrates just how specific certain skills can be. In this case employees were simply moved from one seat in the cockpit to another, yet as a group they went from being excellent performers, albeit on a downward slide, to being totally inept. That sort of problem can occur in training situations: employers know it, workers know it, and businesses adapt to it. Only the government remains resolutely ignorant of it.

Different Investment Pay-offs and the Problem of Cross-subsidies

Even if we assumed that the performance level of different age groups was identical, we would still be confronted with the problem of the anticipated pay-off to a firm for investing in a worker. When a competent company hires a young worker, it knows how to structure its compensation arrangements to maximise its chances of keeping that person for a lengthy period. If a firm does the job properly, today's investment in human resources might be paid back over a period of three or five or seven or ten years. But if a company hires a 65-year-old and makes the same investment, the risk that the person will suffer a health problem soon after and leave the workforce is obviously greater. The rate of return could fall considerably if the period during which the investment is repaid were to be suddenly truncated.

This problem is not confined to firms. It is also a problem constantly faced by universities now that mandatory retirement has been removed. No PhD student wants to sign on with a thesis supervisor who is 75 years old. At best, four or five years down the track that person will be 79 or 80, while at worst they will be retired in Miami or perhaps dead. The student will be left high and dry with a thesis that cannot be completed if another supervisor cannot be found. Of course there are risks with a younger thesis adviser (such as their moving to another university), but they are much smaller. The same situation occurs in any other business. If management has any foresight, it will attempt to plan for the long term. Managers must take into account the likelihood of workers quitting or becoming disabled, and that will increase sharply with age. Here, then, is one area where the new law leads to either irrational investments or to costly attempts to circumvent them.

There are other problems. Wages are typically only part of the total compensation package that a firm provides to a worker. There is also a range of formal and informal benefits, which can often include health insurance as a major component. Nobody would claim that the costs of these benefit packages are invariant to the age of workers. And if companies must pay the same benefit package to somebody aged 70 that they pay to somebody aged 40, and if insurance companies are permitted to discriminate, those insurance companies will charge differential rates. If they cannot discriminate, they may be forced to abandon the entire line of business. It just becomes too risky to accept people at rates that do not allow the companies to cover their costs. Even if insurance companies seek to raise rates uniformly across the board, they will face a serious adverse selection problem because the younger persons who pose lower risks will abandon the system, so that the stated premium will not cover the more substantial risks of the elder persons who remain.

This jostling over rate structures leads to the question of what counts as discrimination, and here the statutes are enormously, and perhaps deliberately, ambiguous. I would prefer to define discrimination as differences in wage levels that do not reflect differences in performance or risk levels. But according to one definition of discrimination, one cannot take risk levels into account. All people are entitled to the same formal benefit for the same work. Thus, age-discrimination statutes effectively lead to enormous and complicated cross-subsidies within a firm. We know what happens when we create internal subsidies. Those people receiving the subsidies will remain with the firm for a long time, while those paying the subsidies will quickly leave. This has serious implications for the firm's long-term viability, not to mention the morale of its workers. It also favours newer firms with younger workforces relative to established firms with older workforces.

Disrupting the Orderly Transition Between Generations

A coherent firm organises itself by planning what we might call an internal firm inheritance. It plans for the transmission of knowledge, skill and managerial talent from one generation to another. One of the great merits of a mandatory retirement rule is that everybody knows roughly when a transition will take place. Younger workers do not sit around restlessly, waiting for arbitrary decisions to be made by senior executives to decide when to go. The senior people know they are leaving. Because they have pride in their business, they apply themselves to training their successors, so that the business can continue to renew itself over time in an orderly manner. Mandatory retirement rules effectively solve the succession problem for businesses in the way elections solve it for democracies. They ensure an orderly turnover.

Suppose that we now interrupt this transition cycle. We say to somebody who is 68 years of age: 'You do not have to retire. If you stay, you will not be engaged in turning this business over to somebody who in two years will be 44'. The tutelage of the younger generation will cease in consequence, because there is no longer any reason for it. The 42 year old will say: 'Why should I stay around indefinitely in a subordinate role? I will chance my luck somewhere else.' Typically, established firms will be handicapped relative to new entrants. New firms will be created by younger people opting out, frustrated at waiting behind their more senior colleagues. So, if statutory prohibitions of mandatory retirement are enforced, I confidently predict that it will shift the balance of advantage between firms. An established business, which once had an edge through its ability to transmit information, will now be at an enormous disadvantage because it will no longer be able to do so efficiently. Most of the people to whom it would have otherwise transferred the information will simply go out on their own. New firms will have an undeserved advantage. It will not result from anything in their human capital or firm culture, but from the peculiar disruption of succession planning in their more-established rivals, another unintended consequence induced by the statute.

We can now see that statutes banning mandatory retirement suffer from two major disadvantages. First, they adversely affect how a firm deals with individual employees. But perhaps more importantly, they change the distribution of age, the transmission of information, and the transmission of control inside the firm in ways that could threaten its very stability. And rational business people will clearly take some countermeasures in response to this legislative intrusion.

A newspaper article written by a thoughtful commentator recently described the new dynamics operating in his business with performance reviews. Under mandatory retirement, if an employee was a year or two within the age of retirement, deterioration in performance was generally overlooked because all parties knew that person would soon be leaving. At present if a manager finds a slight deficiency in performance that enables them to dismiss somebody approaching normal retiring age, that manager will take advantage of it, because the dignified exit afforded by mandatory retirement is no longer available. The statute has given employers a new inducement to find fault with their employees. With automatic retirement, it was not necessary to build up a specific dossier for requiring an employee to leave. But with the mandatory retirement option closed off, an employer has incentives to gather all the dirt on a person in a big folder, and use it to justify a dismissal. Undignified and inhumane procedures substitute for a graceful exit.

All of this must be regarded as an industrial relations catastrophe in the making. And there is no reason for it: that is why we had mandatory retirement policies in the first place. Companies did not have individual case-by-case reviews because everybody understood that the politics involved in deciding exactly how long one person stayed and when another person would go are very ugly. A company would rather see both people go at the same age. Then, if one of them was competent while the other wasn't, that person could be re-hired after retirement. If one firm had a policy of not re-hiring its former employees, some other firm would seize the opportunity. And the firm that released these employees could hire people who were released under mandatory retirement by some other firm.

A firm's mandatory retirement rule is simply a contractual policy. It is not an industry-wide ban on certain individuals. Paradoxically, that rule prolonged the useful working life of people. If workers approaching retirement wanted to continue working, they had a powerful incentive to perform well in their last years at the firm. They were anticipating going back to the market, which meant keeping their skills high. Now that situation is completely reversed.

In universities, the market for older academics has been very important. After the second world war, the University of California essentially built its reputation as a first-rate institution by hiring staff from eastern universities who were in their early-60s and who faced retirement. They chose the best people they could obtain, gave them five-year contracts, and asked them to start a department and hire the next generation of academic staff. These days, if universities employ somebody for a year they may be forced to keep that person for a lifetime. The market for older academics is now dead. This obviously means that universities have to sack non-performers, and that firing people is often fraught with litigation.

Courtroom Follies and Escape Routes

In the United States it is extremely difficult for an employer to win age discrimination cases. Generally they must demonstrate some incompetence in the employee. But an employer typically has two factors in mind when assessing a specific worker's future. One factor is overt instances of incompetence. The other, which the employer knows but is not permitted to articulate, is the tendency for a person's skills to ebb slowly as they age. It happens to baseball players, to computer programmers and even to law professors. If this is indeed a general tendency, the attitude of an employer will simply be to dismiss an employee, perhaps with a pension or an elaborate send-off, before their skills deteriorate too far. They would rather obviate the problem through an orderly transition.

But when such a dismissal case ends up in court, and the employer offers evidence that on average the productivity of a 72-year-old male is only, say, 84 per cent of that of a 66-year-old male, the employer will lose. All evidence must relate to the specific individual in question, and this requirement leaves employers with a huge problem. Typically it is not spectacular under-performance that leads an employer to want to release a worker. It is the employer's general understanding of the path on which that person is travelling. The courts and statutes essentially say that not everything that is known about the situation can be used. For example, the general trends in employment markets are deemed irrelevant. Only facts about aging with respect to a specific worker are legally relevant. Reliance on general trends is assumed to indicate irrational prejudice.

In other words, anybody who is a good probabilistic calculator, or who simply has learnt the lessons from long-term experience, must disregard this entire class of evidence. Instead, any evaluator must concentrate on a single employee in isolation on the grounds that every worker is potentially an exception to any general rule. But it will never be the case that the longshots will always come home, or that the exceptions will prove more important than the rule. Cognitive psychologists remind us constantly of the dangers of disregarding base rate evidence. The age discrimination laws, far from countering that bias, reinforce it.

Notwithstanding this bleak picture, there are three rays of hope, at least in some businesses, for offsetting the worst side-effects of the age discrimination law. First, workers sometimes wish to retire early. To the extent that there is voluntary agreement on retirement, the problem is no longer the age-discrimination statute. Rather, it is the cost of the superannuation schemes that will be incurred, either publicly or privately, to fund an ever-longer retirement. If other things are held constant, any worker demand for early retirement should ease the pressures on the firm.

Secondly, in some countries anti-discrimination statutes contain exemptions for senior employees. In the United States, accruing a sufficiently large pension entitlement allows a person to be forced to leave the firm at a given age. The costs to the firm of the wrong person remaining in a position are much higher with top management than with ordinary employees. For that reason, a board of directors will be more eager to retain their capacity to replace their chief executive at age 65 than to remove other employees. This standard industry practice demonstrates the mythical nature of the common contention that labour markets are characterised by inequality of bargaining power. In this case, a chief executive does not have the power to obtain in their contract an element that is possessed by the employee on the most lowly salary. The obvious explanation: efficiency motivations drive ordinary contractual negotiations at every level in the firm.

A third response is to buy off employees by paying their pensions twice. In the United States, employees are sometimes given large sums of money on the understanding that they will go quietly and waive any claims under the law for unjust dismissal. The legal validity of many of these agreements is unclear. If an employer wishes to avoid a charge of coercion, much will depend upon the correct handling of all the formalities, and the structure of these deals is now a major issue. Inevitably, a policy of providing a buy-out at the end of a person's working life will impact on a firm's ordinary pension scheme. Since employers cannot simply conjure up new funds out of thin air, the new level of bargaining will inject an element that could leave many employees with less income security than they would have had under the previous contractual regime.

Conclusion: Do Not Tinker

Government tinkering with the employment relations system is fraught with pitfalls, no matter how benevolent the intentions of legislators are to improve the lot of working individuals. Legislators cannot change just one element of a system that they regard as irrational, leave all else untouched, and expect everything to go on as before. As with every other type of contract subject to government interference, quite the opposite occurs. Changing a single term that is central to a long-term employment relationship will lead to private adaptations that will change much else as well. The problem may be especially hard to see because the new changes could take place in dimensions that previously were regarded as settled: offices, training, trips, or perks of all sorts could be called into play for no apparent reason, as employers and employees seek to establish a new equilibrium while subject to the legislative command.

The basic moral is that people in all walks of life optimise subject to constraints, even when they are not consciously aware of what they are doing. If a constraint changes or disappears, then the patterns that result from the process of optimisation will also change. This is learnt in the workplace, as a reality confronting managers every day of their professional lives, and not just espoused by academic economists as an interesting theoretical possibility.

Regrettably, in today's climate of opinion, it takes courage to articulate this view publicly. It is senior executives who must fight this policy, yet they are the very people who in the short run are most likely to benefit from an age-discrimination law. That is a great irony. I hope British business people will prove stronger at opposing this law than their counterparts in the United States.

3

Laissez Faire and
Anti-discrimination Laws

There is today a widespread consensus in favour of anti-discrimination laws. That consensus makes it both odd and necessary to ask this question: do anti-discrimination laws create more injustices than they solve?

In order to answer that question it is necessary to have some sense of the landscape, which in broad outline is much the same in the United States as in the United Kingdom, even if the terminology differs in the two places. The 'easy' case of discrimination goes by the name of disparate treatment in the United States, and is called, less informatively, 'direct' discrimination in the United Kingdom and the European Union. The 'hard' case of discrimination goes under the name 'disparate impact' in the United States and 'indirect' discrimination on the Eastern side of the Atlantic. The former involves cases, where from good motive or from ill, a different standard of treatment is applied to men and women, or to individuals of different races, ages and nationalities, where the ground of discrimination is regarded as invidious or illegitimate, especially against members of a protected class. Disparate impact cases result when neutral laws have a larger and more adverse impact against the members of one group compared with another.

The disparate treatment laws are regarded as the paradigmatic cases of wrongdoing for which it is not possible to find any social justification. The disparate

Based on a speech made by Professor Epstein at a conference 'The Regulation of the Workplace: Has It Gone Too Far?', jointly organised by Civitas and the Manhattan Institute at The Armourers' Hall, London, 10 July 2001.

impact standard is meant to backstop the disparate *treatment* standard by allowing the legal system to pierce through the ostensible rationale for some distinction (e.g. a height requirement for police officers) to show that it is a disguised effort, without justification (e.g. safety), to discriminate, even imperfectly, against members of one group (such as women) for the benefit of men. Clearly, the benefits of striking down neutral standards are smaller than those from knocking out explicit standards if only because some members of the under-represented class will meet or exceed the standard: some women will be taller than 5 foot 10 inches. Yet at the same time knocking out the distinction will be more costly because the requirement may well help all workers to do their jobs more effectively (e.g. a police officer may be able to see over crowds for traffic control).

The key question is whether this edifice makes sense. In order to show that it does not, I shall move along the hard road. I shall argue that disparate treatment theories of discrimination are misguided, at which point disparate impact standards fall of their own weight. In America anti-discrimination laws stress 'disparate impact' on ethnic groups. The same doctrines are behind the UK's 'direct' and 'indirect' discrimination. The philosophical justifications are the same.

My criticisms are somewhat unconventional. When I wrote *Forbidden Grounds*[1] I concluded that the United States 1964 Civil Rights Act—which many feel embodies a genuine liberal position—was a mistake and should be repealed. The common law provides a better framework because it allows people freely to enter into mutually acceptable bargains. The argument is simplicity itself. The greatest protection that any prospective worker or customer enjoys comes from the ability to choose his or her trading partners. The law deals best with discrimination by increasing the number of active players in the market. At this point it does not matter whether many or even most people wish not to deal with a given person. The prices and wages in the market place are determined by the contracts made by those, working at the margin, who are eager to deal.

Open markets are consistent not only with invidious discrimination, but also with colour-blind behaviour, and with various outreach and affirmative action programmes. It is decentralised control that creates this richness of opportunity, from which all can benefit.

Let me go back to a larger question. How do we figure out the boundaries between public and private action? What are the limits of state coercion? On that question I am an unreconstructed defender of *laissez faire*. That is not an argument for anarchy, but what do I mean when I say that? The argument starts with a (rebuttable) presumption against government interference in the setting of the terms and conditions of private contracts.

We should be reluctant to invoke state power for two main reasons. First, it is costly for the state to direct actions against people. Second, the state has monopoly power which cannot easily be overcome, short of civil war. This power can be abused.

But the presumption is not conclusive. When can it be overridden? To defend *laissez faire* is not to defend anarchy. Yet since the presumption is not conclusive, areas of state power remain. Some people use private force at the expense of others. This is not tolerable and we are all generally better off living under rules requiring the mutual renunciation of violence. *Laissez faire* is a system of social relations, not a system which asserts the rights of the individual over everything else. It tries to suppress private activity which coerces others and to encourage voluntary actions and voluntary co-operation which make all of us better off. It is not a reckless type of 'possessive' individualism in which everyone is free to do whatever they want.

What behaviour can rightly be controlled? Certainly the use of force comes first on the list, but also right after it comes fraud or deception. The underlying insight is that when individuals enter into voluntary exchanges both parties benefit or the exchange would not be entered into at all. This is a distinctly social conception of right and wrong conduct that does not square with greedy or selfish behaviours.

That said, voluntary exchange falls short in two main areas: infrastructure and private monopoly. Take infrastructure: a road may need to be built across a piece of land and one owner can hold out for a very high price at the expense of everyone else. In such cases compulsion may be necessary, which may be used so long as reasonable compensation is paid so that all taxpayers benefit and the public gain does not force one person to bear the brunt of progress by sacrificing his own property for the good of the whole.

Monopoly is a transactional nightmare, so that state action to limit monopoly power is justified. But what about the employment relationship? There is no monopoly here; only a set of management imperatives. An employer must worry about the morale and motivation of employees. The employment relationship is complex partly because the employer is also the agent of other workers. For example: should a minority of smokers be allowed to smoke in a room shared by many non-smokers?

In the light of these one-on-many interactions, the common model of the dominant employer and the hapless employee does not represent reality. Employers recognise that the interests of the firm are best advanced by happy workers. The employer has the power to discipline, but employees can leave when discipline is misdirected. This exit option is a real threat, which is made more credible when other jobs are open. There is no forced labour. Where there is a free choice of workplace the government's role should be confined to enforcing contracts, not to forcing associations that may not work because of the reluctance of one side to pair up with the other.

What of the criticism that contracts may not root out discrimination? In some cases the point has force. Discrimination creates trouble when a firm possesses monopoly power. Consequently the state should not create or sanction any kind of monopoly. Among the great mistakes of recent times has been the encouragement of labour trade-union monopolies—in such cases governments are forced to introduce a new set of safeguards in order to control the very peril that they have created.

Nor is there any reason to intervene because most forms of bad employer behaviour are self-limiting. An employer does not want to get a bad reputation for discrimination. Reputation is thought to be a weak regulator but its effects can be huge. A company with a bad reputation will not last. Losses will be suffered by shareholders and there will be a reluctance by consumers to buy its products. What if McDonalds announced that it would have no women in its senior management? How long would it be before it was unable to attract able men to work for it? Market pressures tend to encourage non-discrimination. But there will be outliers—perhaps fundamentalist employers who want all workers to take part in morning prayers. Why should we be so confident of our judgement that we feel entitled to shut them down? There is a powerful degree of intolerance behind the wish to use force so freely. There is nothing glorious about using state power to prevent the continued existence and viability of fringe groups.

But you may retort: Epstein, you are naïve! What about extremists? If there is no anti-discrimination law, all those motivated by hatred will get away with it. But what is likely to happen? There will be workforce segmentation; they, the bad apples, will tend to concentrate in one place. My argument is that, whether the motives of the outliers are noble or base, workplace segmentation will be less harmful than the use of force to outlaw it. What, for example, if the enforcement agency itself becomes intolerant and does not represent the majority view? The point here is far from idle because there are no competitive forces to constrain the operations or the excesses of equal or fair employment commissions. Lord Acton's dictum about absolute power can be as true of government agencies today as it was of monarchies when he wrote.

What about promotion at work and the place of qualifications? One argument is that all promotions should be based on independent tests of merit. Examinations allow people to shine regardless of their accent or physical appearance. Such tests are useful and employers should, of course, be allowed to rely on them as necessary if they see fit: after all they have no incentive to give these tests inordinate weight if they are imperfect predictors of future success. However, when you are putting together an institution, abstract measures of merit are not enough. How do people interact? What about the highly-qualified rotten apple? A person with the highest qualifications may be a poisonous presence in an office. When an employer looks at people, he needs to figure out all the intangibles. Regulators merely enforce their own view, but they do not have the ultimate responsibility to make the organisation work. Matters such as morale, which are evident in the workplace, will often escape their attention.

Workplaces vary. In one market it may be best if the workforce is all female, or all male, or all one race or highly cosmopolitan. Knowledge of what works best is likely to be found in local managers, not external regulators. The best outcomes will result when the state enforces contracts only and lets people make their own arrangements.

The law bans disparate treatment, and it also bans neutral treatment which has a disparate impact. As I noted before this expansion of the law comes with higher costs and lower benefits, even when tested against the anti-discrimination norm that underlies disparate treatment cases. It cannot be assumed that regulations will always hit the intended target. Often they do not. If you wish to create opportunity the best rule is: don't worry about *equal* opportunity if that quest will reduce *overall* opportunity. It will make it harder in some cases for members of protected classes to be hired, because it is harder to fire them once on the job. So avoid the pitfalls. Concentrate on eliminating barriers in order to create opportunity for all.

Once that is done, it could well be that some employers, for a variety of reasons, will choose to adopt affirmative action programmes. Well and good. But again, misguided public policy is the upshot if a good practice is converted into a state command. No one quite knows what an affirmative action policy is. Laws can ensure free entry, but not a guaranteed access position. When they aim too high, they fail to hit their target. As in all walks of life, good intentions do not a sound programme make.

Equality, Non-discrimination, and the Labour Market: a Commentary on Richard Epstein's Critique of Anti-discrimination Laws

Simon Deakin

1. Introduction

In his book *Forbidden Grounds* and in a number of related papers, Richard Epstein mounts a powerful case against anti-discrimination legislation. The essence of his case is that discrimination is best dealt with by the market. Legislation which interferes with freedom of contract in the name of equality will simply end up blocking market forces and making matters worse. This is not an argument for the state doing nothing. Governmental action to suppress private coercion and encourage voluntary cooperation may well be legitimate. The state also has a role in attacking monopoly. However, in Epstein's view, none of this justifies the range of anti-discrimination legislation which we currently see in the USA, Britain, and most of mainland Europe. On the contrary, this legislation is part of the problem, which governments would address if they were serious about supporting the market.

In this commentary, I wish to focus on the relationship between equality laws and the market. Contrary to Epstein's argument, I aim to show that the non-discrimination principle supports the market. For individuals to participate in the market, it is necessary that they should have the civil capacity to hold property and enter into contracts. However, these classic liberal rights are not sufficient to ensure effective economic participation. In themselves, they cannot prevent forms of inequality and social exclusion which diminish the scope of the market and threaten its existence. A market which benefits only a minority of society cannot ultimately be sustained. That is why the debate about anti-discrimination law has such resonance in our societies today. It is precisely the spread of the market principle in societies such as Britain and the USA which has led to demands for the expansion over time of anti-discrimination law. This process has not consistently brought about the desired results; indeed, anti-discrimination legislation may not always be the best means of dealing with social exclusion. However, we are more likely to make a reasoned assessment of the advantages and disadvantages of anti-discrimination legislation, and of its possibilities and limits, if we understand that it operates in a close relationship to the market, rather than being fundamentally opposed to it.

I develop my argument as follows. Section 2 is concerned with the kinds of legal institutions which are needed if markets are to function. Here I argue that while Epstein rightly concedes that markets do not operate in a legal vacuum, he has not offered us convincing reasons to believe that a minimal, private-law system of contract and property rights is enough for them to operate effectively. This is because a system of private law is compatible with the persistence of forms of inequality and exclusion which will ultimately undermine the market. The non-discrimination principle addresses this issue by providing for *substantive market access*, going beyond the idea of *formal market access* which is found in private law. Section 3 examines in a wider context the case for and against freedom of contract in employment relations. There I suggest that the presence of externalities and market failures often provides a legitimate basis for legislation regulating the employment relationship, and that such legislation, rather than denying the market, often works in conjunction with market mechanisms, such as reputation and exit, to enhance economic welfare. A number of examples from employment and discrimination law are discussed. Section 4 concludes.

2. Markets, Institutions and Inequality

It is worth briefly restating the case in favour of allowing a substantial role for the market in allocating resources in relation to employment and other spheres of social activity, if only because the case often goes by default. One way of putting it is to say that the market, through free exchange, allocates scarce resources to their most highly valued uses. This is said to be efficient in the sense of satisfying the subjective preferences of market actors to the greatest extent possible. If we take society's welfare to consist of the aggregate of the welfare or well-being of all its members, the allocation achieved through exchange under conditions of perfect market competition cannot be improved on. To that extent, it is an objective to be aimed for, with the support of the law where necessary.

This rather technical explanation, derived from welfare economics, is perhaps something of a diversion from the real issue, which is about decentralisation and individual autonomy versus centralised direction. The market is thought to be advantageous because individual actors know best what their own preferences are. When individuals trade, they generate information about their own wants and endowments which is then available to others. In this sense the market is a mechanism for releasing information and resources which are privately held, in such a way as to benefit all those who participate in the process of trade. The information and resources which are generated this way are immensely more rich than those which would be available to a central planner charged with the task of distributing resources on the basis of assumed needs or political priorities.

Thus, as Epstein says, a market is a form of social order. The right to participate in it is basic to the well-being of individuals; those excluded are fundamentally disadvantaged. At the same time, the more individuals take part in the market system, the greater the overall wealth and/or well-being of the society in question. There is therefore a coincidence between the self-interested behaviour of market actors, and the common good.

However, the conditions for this coincidence cannot
necessarily be guaranteed. The market contains elements
of spontaneous order or equilibrium, but it rests on institutions which may well not be spontaneous, and whose
existence cannot be taken for granted. In the words of
Ronald Coase, 'if self-interest does promote economic
welfare, it is because human institutions have been designed to make it so'.[1]

What then are the institutions on which the market
rests? Epstein rightly points to the importance of the law of
property, contract and tort, or private law. Here he is
writing in a long tradition, traceable to the work of Hayek
and, before that, of Hume. The argument can be para-
phrased as follows. Private law respects the autonomy of
individual action. Property rights ensure that returns
accrue to those responsible for making the relevant investments. Contracts vitiated by force, fraud and deception will
not be granted legal support, but, otherwise, agreements
will be enforced according to their own terms. Tort law
serves to protect existing property and contract rights
against interference, thereby further supporting the system
of exchange. The guarantee of equal protection under the
law, and in particular access to civil capacity to enter into
contracts and hold property rights, ensures that markets
are open to those who wish to trade in them. Private
manipulation of markets should be dealt with by antitrust
law so as to maintain the integrity of the competitive
process.

Those who make the case for a private law system of this
kind do not deny that it may lead to inequalities of wealth
and well being. However, this is not necessarily a problem.
The market provides its own solution since inequalities
incentivise those who, by misfortune or otherwise, fail to
profit from the system. Even if certain gains and losses
accrue by chance, leaving some with what Hayek calls
'undeserved disappointments',[2] the law should not intervene, ex-post, to redistribute resources, since this would
blunt incentives for individuals to invest in their own skills
and efforts.

In my view, it is right to see markets as resting on legal foundations—or, at least, to see markets and the legal system as linked components of a wider social order based around the division of labour and voluntary co-operation. But the close association made in classical liberal thought between the market order and private law usefully highlights certain inherent limits of the market. The market is good at meeting one particular type of objective, namely satisfying those wants or preferences which can be encapsulated in property rights. Conversely, the market will not provide well in relation to those wants or preferences for goods for which no property rights exist. In particular, it fails to work well in relation to so-called 'non-excludable public goods' or 'indivisible commodities', which as a result often end up being supplied by the state or by a non-market source such as a private monopoly.

Equally, the argument for markets is affected by the existence of externalities, or unwanted third party effects. The market enables individuals to make mutually-agreed exchanges with others; but this only satisfies wants *in general* if each transaction affects only those who are party to it. If there are externalities, then transactions between some parties affect the opportunities of others to satisfy their wants. While it is not obvious that state intervention is always the answer, as the 'Coase theorem' recognises,[3] it should be acknowledged that there may well be some scope for intervention, given that the market is not necessarily self-correcting.

But we can go further than this. For the market to operate as a socially useful institution, it is necessary not simply to have a system of property rights, but for individuals to have *endowments* in the sense of items of value which are tradable—as Robert Sugden puts it, 'the market has a strong tendency to supply each person with those things he wants, provided that he owns things that other people want, and provided that the things he wants are things that other people own'.[4] In other words, the market has no inbuilt tendency to satisfy the wants of those who do not have things that other people want.

The implications for our understanding of the relationship between inequality and the market are considerable. Persistent inequalities mean that groups and individuals may lack the resource endowments to enter the market in a meaningful way. In an extreme case, the market will destroy itself unless these negative effects are counter-acted by non-market institutions in the form of regulation and redistribution. In a less extreme case, the market order will continue to function, but will fail to provide adequate economic opportunities for an increasingly large segment of the population. Even if the market survives in this attenuated form, society as a whole is worse off than it would be if access to the market were widened.

Perhaps this is not a problem, since the market is doing nothing more than reflecting the inherited endowments of the individuals concerned. If they have nothing to bring to the market in terms of skills and aptitude for work, no amount of redistribution will improve the terms of trade available to them. However, observation strongly suggests that the ability to trade in the labour market depends on more than the simple genetic endowments of individuals. Access to education, training, and membership of wider support networks, including family ties, are also among the relevant factors. Unequal access to the resources which individuals need in order to enhance their human capital can have a self-reinforcing effect, worsening the position of the disadvantaged to the point where they are excluded from active participation.

In this context, social rights can be seen as the institutional form of those *capabilities* which Amartya Sen argues are the condition for the effective mobilisation by individuals of the resources at their disposal. Sen refers to 'the concept of "functionings" [which] reflects the various things a person may value doing or being. The valued functionings may vary from elementary ones, such as being adequately nourished and being free from avoidable disease, to very complex activities or personal states, such as being able to take part in the life of the community and having self-respect.' Within this context, a 'capability' is 'a kind of freedom: the substantive freedom to achieve alternative functioning combinations'.[5]

Capabilities, therefore, are a consequence not simply of the endowments and motivations of individuals, but also of the access they have to the processes of socialisation, education and training which enable them to exploit their resource endowments. By providing the conditions under which access to these processes is made generally available, mechanisms of redistribution may be not just compatible with, but become a precondition of, the operation of the labour market.

An example may illustrate this point. A conventional economic view of laws which protect women against dismissal on the grounds of pregnancy[6] would be as follows. From the viewpoint of enterprises which would otherwise dismiss pregnant employees once they become unable to carry on working normally, such laws impose a private cost. These enterprises may respond by declining to hire women of child-bearing age who will, as a result, find it more difficult to get jobs. If this happens, there may be an overall loss to society in terms of efficiency, because resources are misallocated and under-utilised, as well as a disadvantage to the women who are unemployed as a result.

An alternative way of thinking about discrimination against pregnant workers is as follows. In the absence of legal protection against this type of discrimination, women of child-bearing age will not expect to continue in employment once (or shortly after) they become pregnant. It is not necessary for all market participants to make a precise calculation along these lines; rather, a norm or convention will emerge, according to which pregnant women expect to lose their jobs and their employers expect to be able to dismiss them without any harm attaching to their reputation. The overall effect is that investments in skills and training are not undertaken, making society worse off as a result. Women workers will have an incentive not to make relation-specific investments in the jobs which they undertake. In an extreme situation, they may withdraw from active participation from the labour market altogether, and norms may encourage this too—as in the case of the 'marriage bar' norm, according to which any woman who married was expected thereupon to resign her position. This norm was widely observed in the British public sector up to the 1950s and, in the case of some local authorities, was even enshrined in legally binding regulations.

What is the effect of the introduction of a prohibition on the dismissal of pregnant women under these circumstances? In addition to remedying the injustice which would otherwise affect individuals who are dismissed for this reason, a law of this kind has the potential to alter incentive structures in such a way as to encourage women employees to seek out, and employers to provide training for, jobs involving relation-specific skills. The demonstration effect of damages awards against employers may over time lead to a situation in which the norm of automatic dismissal is replaced by its opposite. Stigma attaches to those employers who flout the law. As more employers observe the new norm as a matter of course, it will tend to become self-enforcing, in a way which is independent of the law itself. Conversely, more women will expect, as a matter of course, to carry on working while raising families, in a way which may have a wider destabilising effect on the set of conventions which together make up the 'traditional' household division of labour between men and women.

Pregnancy protection laws, therefore, can be seen as a form of institutionalised capability. In other words, they provide the conditions under which, for women workers, the freedom to enter the labour market becomes more than merely formal; it becomes a substantive freedom. This example illustrates the effect which social rights may have in terms of widening market access.

3. Competition and Regulation as Forces Shaping the Employment Contract

A possible response to the claim just made is that it is not in the interests of employers to engage in socially wasteful discrimination. The market system punishes employers who discriminate, by harming their reputation. Moreover, employees have economic power, in the form of the right to exit the employment relationship where they perceive themselves to be subject to unfair treatment. Richard Epstein makes these points as part of his argument for freedom of contract in employment relations in general and for the common law institution of 'employment at will' in particular.

But how effective are extra-legal sanctions in inhibiting employers from acting opportunistically? The option of quitting is not necessarily available to employees who have valuable economic assets—'firm specific human capital'—tied up in their jobs. Jobs are not always interchangeable, and searching for an alternative may be costly. Labour and skills cannot be stored, so that few employees can afford to be without employment for long. As a result, for reasons recognised long ago by Adam Smith:

> it is not difficult... to see which of the two parties must, upon all occasions, have the advantage in the dispute and force the other into compliance with his terms... Many workmen could not subsist a week, few could subsist a month, and scarce any a year, without employment. In the long run, the workman may be as necessary to his master as his master is to him; but the necessity is not so immediate.[7]

Nor is it clear that employers who act harshly or unfairly to employees will suffer adverse reputational effects. There are often severe problems over the quality of information surrounding dismissals, and difficulty in verifying the conflicting claims made by the parties to employment disputes.

This is one reason why we see legislative intervention in the employment relationship. In many jurisdictions, including Britain (although not the USA), employment protection laws offer solutions to some of the very problems of ineffective sanctions and imperfect information which law and economics scholars identify with legal regulation of employment. Unfair dismissal law,[8] for example, is asymmetrical, in the sense that while it circumscribes the employer's sanction of dismissal, it in no way limits the employee's right to quit. *If*, as Epstein suggests, the employee's right to quit is an important means of controlling employer abuse, this possibility is not affected in any way by the enactment of a just cause standard for dismissal. At the same time, unfair dismissal litigation can be a highly effective way of generating information about employer opportunism. Employers with reputations to lose may think twice about acting in breach of commonly-accepted standards when the effects of doing so will be ventilated in a tribunal hearing.

Similar considerations apply in the context of the non-discrimination principle. The conventional economic understanding is that the market itself provides the cure for supposed discrimination. Employers with a 'taste' for discriminating, in hiring and employment decisions, on the grounds of sex or race, will incur a cost in terms of their reduced ability to hire and retain the most efficient workers. Other employers will see an opportunity to hire women and/or members of ethnic minorities at rates of pay which more accurately reflect their true productivity. Over time, these more productive firms will either prevail over their competitors in the market for services or products, or the latter will switch their strategy. In a free market, then, market forces will ensure equal pay for work of equal value prevails without the need for intervention.

However, in practice employers cannot costlessly make reliable estimates of the productivity of individuals before hiring them; nor can they costlessly observe individual effort and link it to output once the employment relationship has begun, thanks to the team-production nature of many tasks. This is one reason why employers tend to use gender and race 'proxies' for individual productivity. This tendency is reinforced if the practice of differentiation on such grounds becomes widespread. Conventions of job segregation, once they arise in this way, can become locked-in and resistant to change even when it is obvious to employers that they may be essentially arbitrary. It may not be in the interests of any one employer to depart from the convention, given that they expect all other employers to follow it. If this is the case, there can be no expectation that spontaneous market forces will necessarily bring about the elimination of social discrimination.

Numerous empirical studies of occupational segregation have identified 'crowding' effects, as the jobs which are 'conventionally' done by women tend to be separated off from those seen as jobs for men, with similar effects operating at the level of discrimination between different ethnic and racial groups. Using the very same job evaluation techniques which employers introduced, initially, as part of the bureaucratic management and control of labour, academic studies and, from the 1980s in Britain, investigations by experts appointed by employment tribunals, have time and again shown that the 'objective' content of jobs is very incompletely correlated with the comparative pay and employment conditions of those who hold them.

Richard Epstein nevertheless argues that the most resistant forms of discrimination are those practiced by employers in a monopoly or near-monopoly position, in particular public bodies and utilities. It is certainly true that defendants in a number of landmark discrimination cases have been governmental bodies or public utilities. As product markets are deregulated and opened up to competition, even within the core of the public sector itself, can we confidently expect the scope for persistent employment discrimination to diminish?

In my view, there are good reasons to believe that competition alone will not succeed in shifting deeply rooted assumptions and perceptions of the comparable worth of particular workers based on their sex and race. Often, the causes of inequality are 'endogenous' to the market in the sense of arising from the impossibility of perfect contracting over the terms of the employment relationship, rather than simply being imposed from outside by artificial conditions of monopoly or by collusion between employers and protected groups.

The root of unequal treatment between men and women in the labour market remains the uneven division of household labour. In households where the large part of (unpaid) domestic work is undertaken by women, a positive externality is created for society as a whole which also shapes, for the worse, the conditions in which women enter (or re-enter, after childbirth) paid employment. This is the origin, in turn, of practices which tend to undervalue female labour. Legal intervention based on the equality principle is necessary to destabilise institutionalised forms of discrimination which would otherwise remain well entrenched. In practice, this may involve the law working with the grain of market mechanisms such as reputation; litigation is a good way of imposing reputational costs upon employers reluctant to give up discriminatory practices.

The principle of 'disparate impact' or 'indirect discrimination' which can be traced back to the decision of the US Supreme Court in the *Griggs* case[9] is of paramount importance, since it enables a court to open up to scrutiny practices whose effects may be long-lasting and far-reaching but which are all the more difficult to challenge because they have the appearance of neutrality. In the USA, the principal context for the application of the 'disparate impact' principle has been race discrimination; in the EC and UK context, it has been sex discrimination. The European Court of Justice's judgment in the *Bilka-Kaufhaus*[10] case in 1986 was a turning point for UK law in that it expressed a wide view of indirect discrimination and incorporated a proportionality test which not only shifted the burden of justification on to the employer but set a high hurdle in terms of the need to show that a particular practice served a legitimate objective while entrenching as little as possible on the equality principle. The seed planted in *Bilka Kaufhaus* blossomed in the House of Lords' decision almost a decade later in 1994 in *R. v. Secretary of State for Employment, ex parte EOC*.[11] Here the House of Lords decided, firstly, that the rule which required part-time workers to be employed for eight or, in some cases, 16 hours a week, before they could begin to qualify for statutory rights in respect of termination of employment, was indirectly discriminatory, since over 80 per cent of part-time workers adversely affected by the rule were women. Secondly, it was held that no effective justification defence had been offered. The government had been content to argue a conventional economic defence to the effect that to include part-time workers in protective legislation would increase the cost of hiring and reduce employment opportunities for this group. This argument was rejected in the House of Lords on the grounds than inadequate evidence had been presented for it, reversing a Court of Appeal ruling in the course of which one judge simply commented that the government's position was 'logical'.

Equally significant was the House of Lords 1995 decision in *Ratcliffe* v. *North Yorkshire County Council*.[12] Here the Council's direct service organisation cut the pay of a group of employees in order to enable it to place a low bid to carry out work which was being put out to competitive tender under the Local Government Act 1988. The Court of Appeal accepted a view that:

> the 'material factor' which led to the lower rates of pay ... was the operation of market forces resulting from the statutory requirement in the 1988 Act that [the employer's] tender could not succeed unless it took full account of those forces.[13]

However, in the House of Lords Lord Slynn argued that the employer was not entitled to make cuts in pay simply in order to compete with an external contractor, which was apparently able to set wages at rates below those set by national collective bargaining by employing only women to do the work in question. While 'conscious of the difficult problem facing the employers in seeking to compete with a rival tenderer', he concluded that to reduce the women's wages below those of their male comparators was 'the very kind of discrimination in relation to pay which the [1970] Act sought to remove'.[14]

In retrospect it would seem that these two decisions were the high point in the UK (to date) of the use of discrimination law to undermine institutionalised inequality in the labour market. Almost as the House of Lords was deciding *ex parte EOC*, the ECJ was hinting, in the *Kirshammer-Hack* case,[15] that there was a margin of discretion for job creation arguments of the kind relied on by the government in *ex parte EOC*, and in a series of later rulings this position hardened to the point where the chances of challenging working hours thresholds which have this exclusionary effect are much diminished.[16] In brushing aside the conventional economic argument for hours thresholds in the way it did, the House of Lords failed to engage with the economic case which might have been made against the thresholds. This is unfortunate, since the economic argument for intervention deserves closer attention.

The implicit thinking behind the 'job creation' argument put forward by the UK government in *ex parte EOC* is that a subsidy is needed to encourage the hiring of part-time workers. This could be because there is a greater administrative burden involved in employing two part-timers rather than one full-timer; if so, a strict approach to the justification defence would require this to be quantified. The more likely explanation is an assumption that part-timers are less productive than full-timers. This, however, seems unlikely; in many cases their productivity is likely to be higher as a result of the reduced hours they work. At the end of the day, the argument that employers need incentives to hire part-time workers on low-hours contracts is little more than a revival of stereotypical assumptions about the comparative worth of male and female labour, assumptions which it is the very purpose of the indirect discrimination principle to expose and challenge.

None of this rules out a role for market forces in eradicating discrimination. My point is simply that we should not place our faith in competition alone. There are many ways in which the law can, and should, aid and where necessary adjust the competitive process. The application of the indirect discrimination principle can unravel persistent forms of discrimination, and may go some way to righting historic wrongs. However, it is reactive in the sense that it can only act on existing practices. A more proactive mechanism for promoting competition in the labour market is affirmative action. It is surprising that this form of intervention has not won more support from law and economics scholars, since it directly encourages competition by breaking down barriers to entry to privileged jobs on the part of groups previously excluded by the effects of conventional or stereotypical views.

Quotas and preferential hiring policies to aid disadvantaged minorities are currently outlawed in the UK, since the principle of direct discrimination (the UK equivalent of 'disparate treatment') is very strictly defined and requires employers to treat individual applications strictly on their merits. In the USA, by contrast, private-sector voluntary affirmative action programmes are permitted where they are designed to remedy conspicuous racial imbalances in an employer's workforce, they are temporary in nature, and they disproportionately interfere with the interests of the majority group of employees (particularly in the sense of preserving accrued seniority rights). In the public sector, employers are frequently required to take affirmative action to recruit, hire and promote women and racial minorities where they had previously been 'under-utilised' in the employer's workforce; these requirements have given rise to an extensive litigation aimed at questioning their constitutionality. In the European context, the ECJ held in *Marschall v Land Nordrhein Westfalen*[17] that a form of affirmative action under which, in a situation of under-representation of female employees, an equally well qualified female applicant would be given preference over a male, did not contravene EC law, as long as the following conditions were met: first, the employer made provision for a 'saving clause' under which it could take into account objective factors which were specific to an individual male; and the criteria involved in such a process were not such as to discriminate against the female candidates. The basis for the Court's ruling, significantly, was that affirmative action was acceptable where it was aimed at counteracting 'the prejudicial effects on female candidates' of stereotypical attitudes and behaviour relating to the roles and capacities of women in working life. Both the Framework Directive on Discrimination and the Race Directive[18] now contain a provision according to which '[w]ith a view to ensuring full equality in practice, the principle of equal treatment shall not prevent any Member State from maintaining or adopting specific measures to prevent or compensate for disadvantages linked to' the ground of discrimination in question. This is a significant step forward, and one which the UK should consider taking advantage of.

4. Conclusions

In this commentary I have argued that the non-discrimination principle has an important role to play in opening up labour markets to disadvantaged groups, thereby extending the scope of the market in such a way as to benefit all market participants. The market is a powerful force for promoting greater equality and for mobilising society's resources, but the market is not self-constituting. It rests on a number of non-spontaneous institutions, of which the legal order is one. While the classical liberal notion of equality—equal civil capacity under the law—is necessary to the elimination of institutionalised disadvantage, it is not sufficient. That is why we have seen an increasing focus on legal notions of equality which stress substantive, and not simply formal, market access. Modern anti-discrimination legislation is the most concrete manifestation of this idea; it is no accident that it has flourished in market economies which stress the importance of labour market participation.

   While my conclusion could not be more clearly opposed to that offered by Richard Epstein, the method I have used is essentially the same as his. We both reject the 'anarcho-capitalist' position which sees no need for a legal order of any kind to support the market, and we both see a role for legal institutions in supporting market mechanisms of reputation, exit and choice. The disagreement lies in the view we take of the difficulties posed by informational symmetries and market failures, on the one hand, and the problems of special pleading and interest-group activities in framing legislative intervention, on the other. In my view, the search for an appropriate ethical basis to the labour market—one which will enhance voluntary co-operation and an extensive division of labour—is on balance assisted, and not impeded, by modern anti-discrimination law.

A Short Reply to Simon Deakin

Richard A. Epstein

I have just read Simon Deakin's thoughtful comments on my earlier criticism of the anti-discrimination laws as they operate in the United States and the United Kingdom, and take this opportunity to comment on the similarities, and differences, in our two positions. Starting with the former, neither Deakin nor I believe that a system of well-functioning markets could arise solely out of the operation of what Hayek has called the 'spontaneous order'. To be sure, it is possible for some markets to operate wholly in the absence of any legal coercion whatsoever, but the general history of commercial endeavours speaks more emphatically towards a different truth. Markets work best when property rights are secured by the state, when contracts are enforced, when fraud and duress are held in check, when monopolies are constrained, and when social infrastructure is available. All this activity takes government action; to create, as Coase suggests, the correct incentives to get the best out of individual self-interest. Within this general legal frame-work, the role for spontaneous order[1]—a phrase that leaves me uneasy—should be best understood as demanding only that the state take no role in deciding (a) who should contract with whom, and (b) what the terms and conditions of their agreements should be.

The anti-discrimination laws in employment take dead aim at both point (a) and point (b). In an ideal world, I see little place for their use. Labour markets are very difficult to monopolise given the possibility of free entry. One common justification for an anti-discrimination principle applies to common carriers—that is, to such operations as rails and waterways, or other network industries such as gas and power, where a supplier enjoys some form of

monopoly status. In those contexts, use of the anti-discrimination norm is rightly justified, as has long been recognised,
as a counterweight to monopoly power. Unregulated labour
markets, in contrast, offer few possibilities for monopolisa-
tion. Ironically, therefore, it is only when the government
affords unions monopoly power over their own workers that
the anti-discrimination principle—which in the United
States travels under the name of the duty of fair-represen-
tation[2]—comes into play. Otherwise, the simple logic of the
market will outperform any effort by the state to limit the
first of the two principles of market order set out above—the
ability of each person or firm to decide with whom to enter
into a contract of employment, and on what terms.

Deakin is wise enough in his critique of markets not to
pretend that they have no advantages in the allocation of
social resources. Rather, he tries to demonstrate that
certain real imperfections remain in markets even after we
acknowledge the government role in supplying public goods
and constraining force, fraud and monopoly. With a nod to
Sen's theory of 'capacity', he articulates this position by
noting that markets may guarantee legal rights to participate in economic activities, but that they do not necessarily
supply *effective* rights of participation (pp. 41 and 46).[3]
Stated otherwise, legal capacity is not social capacity, and
the guarantees of *formal market access* do not carry with
them guarantees of *substantive market access*.

This philosophical claim is far too facile for its own good.
One difficulty is that neither Deakin nor, as far as I can tell,
anyone else, has supplied any definition of what counts as
an effective right of market participation above and beyond
the ability to hold property and enter into contracts. Surely
that term does not carry with it the sense that markets
should be deemed to fail unless all individuals are able to
secure some form of living wage as measured by some
external and objective standard. In any large population,
some portion of the population will fail in economic activities, no matter what legal régime is in place. It becomes,
therefore, something of an impossibility for anyone to make
operational a test for when participation is effective, for

when people with full legal capacities have adequate social capacities.

Worse still, there is no costless way to secure effective participation or substantive market access. Thus any system of subsidies, regulations or prohibitions will not have just the single intended effect of allowing some people to enter into markets from which they were otherwise excluded. A decision, for example, to require any given firm to pay state-designated minimum wages will not just raise the wages of all employed persons who are below that stipulated level, leaving all other features of the economic system unchanged. Some fraction of them may lose their jobs entirely, and others will find that other terms of employment (e.g. levels of job training) are shifted in ways that work to their disadvantage. The overall system of regulation, moreover, could lead to a reduction in the number of jobs made available at all levels by reducing the willingness of firms to enter markets in the first place. We cannot repeal the law of unintended consequences. Efforts to secure effective participation in job markets are often little more than disguised barriers to entry that can easily lead to a reduction in the total amount of opportunities that are available. If one is concerned about the provision of minimum levels of subsistence, as writers like Hayek and Milton Friedman are,[4] then one should think in terms of guaranteed minimum income levels and progressive taxation, even if these are themselves fraught with political difficulties.[5] There is no reason to experiment with a negative income tax to meet that objective.

Deakin spends little time worrying about the fit of the anti-discrimination laws with any perceived failure of market institutions. But, to his credit, he is not content to rest with this broad criticism of market institutions. He also tries to identify some concrete ways in which open markets may well lead to a cycle of inequality and exclusion. He notes that individuals without education will be consigned to the bottom rungs of the market economy, if they can get a toehold at all. However, he does not explain why the anti-discrimination laws are the appropriate antidote. And his selective account of the operation of markets ignores the vast amount of education that firms *do* provide for workers with whom they have formed effective long-term relations. Internal promotion is one of the keys for organising a successful firm. The number of errand-boys and secretaries who have risen to higher positions within the firm is too numerous to count. We pay a high social price when we chop off the bottom rung of the ladder in the name of greater access to market institutions, for the folks who do not get on the ladder at all cannot rise step by step.

The same critique applies to the anti-discrimination laws. Deakin notes that employers who rely on stereotypes often commit a double sin: they disable themselves and they make it harder for members of certain groups to gain access to the market (pp. 50-51). Unfortunately, he misses the explanation as to why there is a greater reliance on these stereotypes than there ought to be: the anti-discrimination laws with their preoccupation with indirect discrimination (the American disparate impact) have made it more costly for firms to acquire particular information about individual workers by barring the use of standard tests that help project the potential career paths of their workers. Once denied this information, there is a *rational* reason to turn to stereotypes. But the cure goes in the opposite direction: it is to allow the full range of employee testing to take place, and then for the market to sort itself out on the strength of those results. If the tests are unreliable, then they will be disregarded with time. But if they are reliable, then the refusal to sanction their use will result in large distortions that will undermine Deakin's stated goal of effective participation in labour markets.

A similar analysis applies to Deakin's argument in favour of state intervention against discrimination on grounds of sex and pregnancy (pp. 47-48). On the larger issue, Deakin starts with the obvious point that even today there is an 'uneven division' in the level of household labour. Women do more work within the home and men do less. Yet by the same token men work longer hours in the workforce than do women. It is wrong, however, to draw from these truisms any inference that this distribution of tasks creates some positive externality for society as a whole which is unacknowledged in a market system. Most obviously, the direct beneficiary of a woman's household labour is the woman herself and her family. To be sure, society benefits from well-ordered households, but that includes all the contributions of both parties to the marriage. So long as husband and wife agree on the allocation of family tasks, the uneven contributions within the household is no social problem. It represents a welcome division of labour within the family that increases the overall productivity of the family unit as a whole. There is no misallocation to be cured.

Deakin holds similarly odd views on the question of pregnancy. Initially, it appears that he does not attach any independent value to the contribution that women make to their families and society by shouldering the bulk of the work in rearing children. Nor is he able to show any market distortion that justifies a prohibition against pregnancy discrimination within the market place. At no point does he acknowledge that, in some circumstances at least, the employment of pregnant women will constitute a cost for the firm. Yet by the same token he does not acknowledge that in some instances firms will be willing to bear these costs. He stresses that some firms might well dismiss women once they are pregnant, but he remains regrettably silent about the huge number of firms that routinely make accommodations to keep pregnant women, or women with young children, on the job: part time hours; job splits; work from home; childcare and the like. None of this is required by the current set of pregnancy discrimination laws, and yet it is offered by firms who are reluctant to lose some of their ablest employees. Clearly we have to chalk these innovations up to market forces.

By the same token, these accommodations might not be available for all pregnant women in all positions. Nor should they be. Some jobs do require people to work 24/7, and, if so, then a vibrant labour market is one that allows women to shift jobs, and not one that tries to tether them to their existing firm when that shift is appropriate. There is really no case of distortion in investments in human capital in an unregulated labour market: once it is clear which opportunities will be available, then women who intend to have children can tailor their career plans to take into account their dual objectives. The pregnancy laws only introduce an undesirable set of cross-subsidies in which all other workers—not only men, but many women as well—are forced to subsidise the decisions of the law's beneficiaries. Their willingness to invest in human capital will be reduced if the promised returns are limited by the anti-discrimination law that favours one fraction of the workforce over another. Once we recognise that it is not possible to form any responsible generalisation about the impact of pregnancy on job performance, it becomes at best mischievous to impose a legal rule that requires all employers to retain pregnant workers against their will.

There is yet another sense in which Deakin is wide of the mark in his endorsement of the status quo in labour markets: his misplaced reliance on Adam Smith (p. 49). Smith clearly did say that workers have necessities in the short-run while employers have them only in the long run, so that the advantage in negotiations lies with the employer. But on this occasion, I think that we have to say that Smith erred. One constant theme of the labour literature is the worker who threatens to walk off the job when the crops are ready to be harvested unless he receives a fat wage increase. At this point the advantage runs decidedly in the opposite direction, unless an employment contract binds the worker. Short-term hold-up problems are not a function of wealth, but of the level of disruption that a strategically designed walk-out can effectuate. The situation is only worse when there is a collective refusal to deal. It is no wonder that unions typically seek to have their contracts terminated when they will cause the firm the maximum amount of disruption.

Nor does Smith's argument take into account the change in relative positions brought about by the greater prosperity of modern times. Higher wage levels imply that workers often have savings and unemployment benefits. Many families have access to credit that can tide them over in the short run, or have both spouses working so as to insulate them from some of the adverse consequences of the lay-off for one. Improved capital markets have aided the position of workers as a class. At the same time, dot.coms by the score failed because they could not get that next infusion of venture capital. It is a hard world out there for all players on both sides of the market. But employers in competitive labour markets are not exempt from heavy pressures in both the long and the short term. There is no systematic advantage for one side over the other. Nor is there any reason to think that an anti-discrimination law provides any antidote to whatever bargaining imbalance that might exist. Quite the contrary, the people who are most hard-pressed, such as single-mothers with little education, will find that the anti-discrimination laws operate as a barrier of entry to them. Ironically, some form of a private affirmative action programme (of which there are many in the United States) might provide some form of a difference, but here, as Deakin reminds us (pp. 54-55), the rules of the EU tend to preclude the private voluntary responses that might have some legs in the long run. Deakin may be right that many law and economics scholars have not seen the potential gains of affirmative action programmes. But I have long championed the right of private firms to engage in affirmative action, not because I am convinced that it is the right thing for all firms to do, but because I think that each firm should be free to decide for itself whether to do it or not.[6] The negation of the principle of freedom of association that is found in the anti-discrimination law operates as a constant thorn in the side of private affirmative action programmes.

In the end, therefore, I see nothing that alters the analysis that I gave earlier of the anti-discrimination laws. The most troublesome problem we have today is that the level of education offered to individuals from disadvantaged markets will not allow them to take advantage of the information economy. But there is nothing that an anti-discrimination law can do to solve this problem unless it treats qualifications as an invidious form of discrimination. To answer that question we have to address candidly the issue of what system of education works best. Why any one would think that a state-run monopoly offers the best solution to this issue eludes me, but that is a topic for another day.

Notes

Richard A. Epstein

1   Epstein, R.A., *Forbidden Grounds: The Case Against Employment Discrimination Laws*, Cambridge: Harvard University Press, 1992.

Simon Deakin

1   Coase, R.H., *The Firm, the Market and the Law*, Chicago: University of Chicago Press, 1988, p. 134. (Coase here paraphrases an argument made previously by A.C. Pigou).

2   Hayek, F.A.,*The Mirage of Social Justice*, London: Routledge and Kegan Paul, 1976, p. 127.

3   Coase, *The Firm, the Market and the Law*, 1988.

4   Sugden, R., 'Spontaneous order', in Newman, P. (ed.), *The Palgrave Dictionary of Economics and the Law*, Vol. III, London: Macmillan, 1998, p. 492.

5   Sen, A., *Development as Freedom*, Oxford: OUP, 1999, p. 75.

6   The relevant protection in UK law is contained in the Employment Rights Act 1996, s. 99, and related provisions.

7   Smith, A., *An Inquiry into the Nature and Causes of the Wealth of Nations*, Book II, (first published 1776) London: Nelson, 1886, p. 26.

8   As contained in the Employment Rights Act 1996, Part V.

9   *Griggs* v. *Duke Power Co.* 401 US 424 (1971).

10   Case 170/84 *Bilka Kaufhaus* v. *Weber von Hartz* [1986] IRLR 317.

11   [1994] IRLR 176.

12   [1995] IRLR 439.

13   [1994] IRLR 342, 363.

14   [1995] IRLR 439, 443.

15   Case 189/91 [[1994] IRLR 185.

16   See Deakin and Morris, *Labour Law*, 3rd edn, Butterworths, 2001, pp. 579-80.

17   Case C-409/95 [1998] IRLR 39.

18   Directive 2000/78, Art 7 and Directive 2000/42, Art 5, respectively.

A Short Reply to Simon Deakin

1   For a discussion see Robert Sudgen, 'Spontaneous order', in Newman, P. (ed.), *The Palgrave Dictionary of Economics and the Law*, London: Macmillan, Vol. III,1998, referred to by Deakin.

2   See, Steele v. Louisville & Nashville Railroad Co., 323 U.S. 192 (1944).

3   See Sen, A., *Development as Freedom*, Oxford: OUP, 1999, p. 75.

4   Hayek, F., *The Constitution of Liberty*, London: Routledge & Kegan Paul, 1960, pp. 285-305; Milton & Rose Friedman,M. And Friedman, R., *Free to Choose*, London: Penguin; New York: Harcourt Brace Jovanovich, 1980, pp. 149-55.

5   See, for my views, Epstein, R.A., *Hayekian Socialism*, 58 Maryland L. Rev. 271 (1999).

6   For discussion, see Epstein, R.A., *Forbidden Grounds: The Case Against Employment Discrimination Laws*, Cambridge: Harvard University Press, 1992, pp. 412-37.